ever♥more

POEMS ON PREGNANCY & MOTHERHOOD

jessica jocelyn

Ever More
Copyright © 2024 Jessica Jocelyn
All rights reserved. No part of this
book may be reproduced or used in any
matter without the written consent of
the copyright owner.
ISBN: 979-8-9879305-6-4

Illustrations: Janelle Parraz
Cover design: Janelle Parraz and
Jessica Jocelyn
Fonts by: saltandpepperfonts

for my mother-in-law
Victoria Ann.
may our souls find each other
again someday

Part 1　1

Part 2　63

welcome to motherhood

motherhood is a journey.
at times it is thankless
and monotonous.
sometimes it feels like an endless cycle
in which you may not sleep again.
you'll run and hide
and eat the good snacks in the closet
or rush into the bathroom
to let out silent screams.
you'll crave time away,
but here's the thing.
once you're away,
you'll miss it.
you'll miss the chaos, the playing.
you'll miss the small hands touching you
and all you'll think about is going back.
your heart will want to explode with love
when you realize you are all they want.
welcome to the most terrifying
and beautiful journey you will ever embark on.

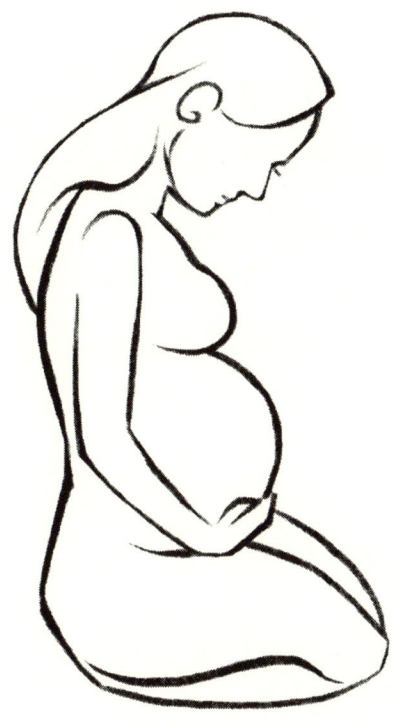

Part 1

jessica jocelyn

as I grew into my adolescence,
I was sure I'd never have children.
both my parents gave up,
each in their own ways
so I wasn't sure it was ever something
that I wanted to do.
to me it was passing on more
then just my dark hair
or maybe my tenacity.
I could possibly birth my wounds
and the wounds of my parents as well.
but then I met a man.
a beautiful, tall man.
I imagined him holding babies
and teaching them to build things.
and maybe it was selfish,
but I wanted nothing more
then to see that,
to raise and teach children with him.
to be the reason
there were more good people
in this world.

not the most cinematic, romantic moment,
but he sat next to me
as I took that test.
I wouldn't have had it
any other way.
as a woman, I knew pregnancy
was a possibility.
but I never thought it would happen to me
until it did.
I had taken many, many tests before,
but all were negative.
but there they were-
bright, strong, instant.
the 2 pink lines.
no way.
no freaking way.
is this real?
he hugged me and we cried,
me still sitting on that toilet.

the doppler is pushing hard
onto my abdomen.
after what seems like an eternity,
she says she can't find the heartbeat
but will try an ultrasound.
my husband squeezes my hand.
"don't worry," he whispers.
the warm goo goes on
and she slides over me with ease.
a loud whooshing fills the room.
for those two minutes,
I am convinced
the world went silent
to make way for the beautiful sound
of that heartbeat.
I can't breathe;
there's my baby.
I just can't believe
that's my whole life
right there on that screen.

I'm not sure
what color your eyes will be,
but I already love you.
I don't know if you will like sports
or if you will be more into the arts,
but I already love you.
I don't know if you'll be tall like daddy
or short like me,
but I already love you.
I'm not always sure of much,
but I know for certain
that I already love you.

I was walking through the living room
and my husband sneezed.
I froze
as it felt like butterflies
were fluttering in my stomach.
it was over
as quickly as it started
and immediately I picked up the phone
and called my mother-in-law.
she laughed and told me she was sure
I had just felt my baby's first kicks.

I wore a flowing blue shirt today.
I have my 20-week scan
and I'm hoping it's a boy.
my husband is holding my hand
and the wand glides over my belly.
2 lungs.
2 kidneys.
the spine looks good.
she asks if we are ready.
I've been ready for a lifetime it seems.

"see that? it's a boy."

my belly is growing in size so my husband takes me shopping to find clothes that are more comfortable. he sits outside the dressing room and goes back and forth as I keep telling him to bring me bigger sizes. we move on to bras and I can't believe how much bigger everything I'm buying is. nothing seems to fit right and I feel so uncomfortable. I sit down and feel the nausea come back. it's a little past halfway through my pregnancy and it still hasn't gone away. I reach for the almonds in my purse and start to cry. my husband hears me crying and knocks and I let him inside the room.

"what's wrong?" he asks.

"I don't want to wear any of this. I feel so uncomfortable; I can't get anything to fit right," I whimper back.

he holds me and suddenly I reach for my purse and pull out a bag. he knows I'm about to throw up, so he reaches for my hair and holds it back. when I'm done heaving, we just sit there and he embraces me while I cry. when I open my eyes again, I catch a glimpse of myself in the mirror. I feel I've been robbed of that "glow" and was just given acne instead.

"I can't do this. I throw up all day, every day. I can fall asleep standing up. I have such a short temper, everything makes me angry."

he hugs me again and whispers in my ear that I'm doing a good job and we sit there until I'm ready to leave.

what I'm doing is such a beautiful thing, but it's hard that parts of it don't reflect the beauty.

with every twist and turn,
I feel you running out of room.
you start to move slower,
almost like you are just as tired as I am.
everything hurts
and I haven't been able to rest.
I sit up all night staring at the moon
and wishing on stars
so that I might fall asleep.
I feel like my body
is just adding the finishing touches to you
as each day that passes feels like years.
is today the day that we finally meet?

I sure hope so.
I'm so ready to meet you.

jessica jocelyn

I wash the tiniest of clothes,
hold small socks in my hand.
I wash all the bedding
while your daddy builds your crib.
our tiny home will no longer be quiet
and soon it will be filled with so much noise.
it will not be just us two anymore,
and one day it will be hard to imagine
what life was like before you.
your daddy takes pictures of me
right before we go to the hospital
and we can't believe that we will
soon be bringing you home.
"I'm so scared," I whisper
as we share one more pregnant hug.
we laugh at how big I've gotten
and how I waddle out the door.

birth mantra

I surrender to this pain.
I'm allowing it to disintegrate
all that I was before.
this is the closest I will come to death
but also when I will feel
the most alive.
my baby will be guided
by my body
and we will move together
until the pain subsides
and the real journey begins.

jessica jocelyn

when the doctor
put you on my chest,
I felt more than just those
eight pounds.
I felt all the weight
of your hopes and dreams.
I felt the heaviness
of how much you would need me.
you were more than just eight pounds;
you were the weight of the world.
my world.
my forever.
my always.
my ever more.

you are placed in my arms,
all bundled and warm.
oh, little one,
I don't know what I'm doing,
but I do know we are going to
figure this out together,
you and I,
side by side,
hand in hand.

it's hard to imagine
where you began.
I feel like you were always here, somehow.
a part of me,
that maybe we'd met before.
but it wasn't until this moment,
as I looked into your eyes
for the first time,
I finally fully understood
what love was.

from a father's eyes

it was the calm after the storm.
I had just watched her body open
and my baby was guided out.
it was now so quiet,
but it was a comfortable silence.
no one dared make a noise
to disrupt the scene going on.
my baby, our baby,
was nestled safely between her breasts
and all I could do was watch
the way he looked at her,
like he had known her
in many previous lives.
she was being stitched up
but was oblivious to it
as all she could do was drink him in.
I would never be able to look at her the same.
she was like a warrior coming back from battle,
carrying home a new world for her people.
I watched her bring life into this world
in an experience that almost felt religious.
I wasn't sure I believed in that sort of thing,
but watching my baby come earth-side
was the definition of a miracle.

you're so tiny.
I'm so scared to change your diaper
for the first time.
what if I hurt you?
I've never changed a diaper this tiny before!
do I get one ready before I do it?
I stand on one side of you
and your daddy stands on the other.
I open your diaper and see the first tarry poop.
I gasp and you start to pee.
my mother-in-law is behind us,
taking pictures and laughing.
she is a seasoned mother
who loves watching all the first moments
and how we learn from our mistakes.
we fumble, but clean you,
and you're now dry and happy.
one diaper down.
7,000 more to go.

you no longer live inside my body,
but I will always be your home.
I will still shelter you
and offer comfort.
when the tears come,
I will be there.

that was easily the scariest
car ride of my life,
but you slept through it all.
we are still deep in the newborn coma phase
as I show you around.
we laugh,
your daddy and I,
as he blows up a donut for me to sit on
and I try to get comfortable,
a feat that's mostly impossible
when sitting on stitches.

you fall asleep on my chest,
and I know I should go to sleep, too.
but instead I watch you.
I touch the soft fuzz on your cheeks
and brush your tiny baby curls
off your forehead.
I try to count the eyelashes
that are now coming in.
I should close my eyes,
but I can't.
I am lost in marveling how
something so perfect
came from someone so broken.
you are the one thing
that I got right.

flutters of life within me
have turned into
the most beautiful thing
I have ever seen,
with 10 small fingers
and 10 tiny toes.
I kiss each one
and breathe in deep.
I want to memorize
the way you smell
right in this moment.

you are a month old.
it's 8:00 in the morning
your daddy is already at work.
we haven't slept.
for the first time since you've been born,
I cry.
I cry for sleep.
I cry for you to sleep.
I'm not sure I can do this.
I text your daddy these words.
in 5 minutes, your grandma is at our front door.
she comes in and grabs you
with hands that have held and raised
many babies.
I run to the bed and don't come back
for 4 hours.
she laughs when I wake up
and tells me stories of your daddy
when he was first born.

I want to show you
all the light in the world
before life has a chance
to show you darkness.

ever more

I feel I was given two lives,
and the second one began
the day you were born.
it was the day I discovered
what true unconditional love was.
and I didn't just want to say
that I would die for you.
I wanted to be able to say
I'd live for you.
I was content on who I was before,
but for you, I needed to be better.
I needed to heal my body,
my heart,
my mind.

jessica jocelyn

I watch you
as you play on the floor-
so content, so happy.
you turn your head and look at me.
you smile and reach for me
with all the yearning in the world.
the way you look at me,
it's like I can almost hear you say:
I need you.
little do you know,
soon enough,
you are all you'll ever need.
you'll soon see that more and more
as you grow and the days go on.
the day you walk into
your first classroom.
the day you learn to drive a car.
the day you find your first apartment.
but for now,
I will get lost in this yearning,
and bring you into my arms.

my beautiful child,
the wars of your mother
will not be yours to bear.
you will never witness
the storms within my soul
or meet the demons
that inhabit it.
you will be sheltered
under my branches
that I have grown just for you,
a brand-new family tree
with all the rot cut out.
you will never be crushed
by the weight that I carry;
you will be carefree,
just as a child should be.

jessica jocelyn

if I could,
I would swallow all the bad
in this world
so
you'd never know sadness and
you'd never know pain.
I would turn all the bad
into so many bright stars
to light up
every dark night you encounter.

I had no idea
I could survive on this little sleep.
how do I keep moving,
keep getting everything done?
my thoughts seem to run together
and the hours are a blur.
newborn cries fill the car,
piercing through my soul.
there's nothing I can do
to help him at the moment.
I'm lost in everything I keep track of
how many bottles,
how many ounces,
the last time he pooped,
the last time I showered.
I don't recognize the girl
staring back at me in the mirror.
and still feel foreign in my own body.
I may never be alone,
but I am the loneliest I've ever felt
in my entire life.

I'm so on edge.
is my baby sleeping enough?
is my baby sleeping too much?
wait...
is my baby breathing?
I rush to the other side of the room
and touch his chest.
I don't start breathing until I'm sure
that he's breathing, too.
I move my hand away.
wait...
did I really feel him breathing?
let me check again.
should I wake him up?
he probably needs to eat.
if he sleeps too much, then he won't sleep
tonight.
what if there's something in this formula
and there will be a recall soon?
maybe I should make the bottle
before I wake him.
he gets so angry waiting for it to be made.
what if all that crying damages his brain?
wait...
is he still breathing?
I gently wake him just to hear his cry.
crying means he's okay, right?

wait...

someone sees me out in public
and asks how I'm doing.

how am I?

when I take showers, I'm convinced I hear my
baby cry the whole time, but he never really is.
I don't want to be touched anymore, but I want
someone to hold me and tell me it's going to be
okay. I feel I am not doing enough and my baby
deserves more than me, someone who is happy
all the time, someone with more energy. I need
help. I want you to come over and do some
laundry for me so I can bond with my baby, but
I can't. I will never ask for help. asking for help
makes me feel weak and I'm supposed to be able
to do this all by myself. I need a break, but I
feel like if I leave my baby, I am not a good
mother, so I never leave him. I check if he is
breathing every 10 minutes after he falls asleep.

but I can't say all of that.
that's not what she wants to hear.

"I'm fine!" I exclaim as I give her a smile.

my baby is still so new with life and starting to really love his baths. he splashes in the bubbles and laughs. all of a sudden, the bathroom floor has become an ocean and the sun is going down. the water is all around us and getting rough. I'm scared and my first thought is: *"I need to protect my baby."*

I reach out to him, but he doesn't seem bothered. he starts to float away from me and I reach out to grab him. I can't get to him. I start to panic. he giggles as his tiny little bath becomes a boat and sails away from me. I'm trying to get to him, but he just keeps getting further and further from me. I feel a hand on my shoulder and I jump.

"are you okay?"

the warmth of my husband's hand grounds me and all of a sudden we are in the bathroom again. there's no ocean, there's no sunset. my baby is in his bathtub, not a boat.

"no," I whisper.
"no, I'm not."

I'm sitting with my therapist
and crying and telling her that
I don't know if my baby likes me.
I describe all the things happening to me,
that I don't know why I'm having
such a hard time
and why I'm crying so much.
I feel like such a bad mother.
we talk about postpartum psychosis
and about all the anxiety I'm feeling
and that I will need help.
I tell her I'm terrified to leave my baby,
but she tells me
that I cannot possibly take care of my baby
if I don't take care of myself.
that what's happening is not my fault,
that hormones drop super quickly after birth.

"when you get on an airplane, they even tell you that you have to put your oxygen mask on first so you can help your child put on theirs. this is you putting the oxygen mask on."

my baby is almost a year old and I don't want to leave him, but I know I need help. I do it for him, and I do it for myself.

my mother-in-law watches him for a week while my husband is at work, and I know he's safe. I go away to get better and when I return, I have the tools to be the best mother that I can be.

therapy and pills,
more pills and therapy.
I grow tired of all the cocktails
thrown at me.
I just want to be okay.
they make me even more tired,
almost numb to the world.
but I don't want to be numb.
I want to cry the sadness away
as much as I want to laugh again.
I can't wait for this storm to be over
so I can enjoy these moments
that I'll never get back.

looking back at pictures
of you as a newborn
absolutely guts me.
because that's me...
and that's definitely you...
but I don't remember
the world having color.
everything was so gray.
I don't remember me smiling.
all I see is a woman
who is desperately struggling
and holding on to a precious gift
convinced she was not good enough to receive.
sometimes, I don't even remember
the moment the picture was taken,
it's all a blur.
I want so badly to hug that woman
in those pictures,
and tell her she is amazing,
that one day she won't feel like this anymore.

as I watch you play so happily,
I can't help but mourn
all the time PPD
took from us.

it's not just your birthday-
it's also the anniversary
of the day you came into my life.
a day I get to reflect
on your birth story,
remembering the weight of you
on my chest,
feeling your warm cheek against mine.
how in those first moments
you were so terrified
until you realized I was there.
you knew my scent, my voice,
and they instantly calmed you.

jessica jocelyn

I remember how I couldn't wait
for you to start walking and talking,
and then I blinked.
the years were slow and fast
at the same time.

grocery pickups were made
for toddler years
and internet shopping
is a much easier choice these days.
the day I surfboard carried
my toddler out of the store
and left a full cart of groceries
was the day I think I earned
a motherhood badge.
I had many eyes on me-
some nodding because they understood
and others shaking their heads
because the shame never stops
being thrown.
as I clean one mess,
he creates another behind me.
I find fingerprints in places
I didn't know he could reach.

things I never want to forget:

- your perfect head on my shoulder for the first time
- your tiny hand reaching for the snack at the drive thru window
- your screams when you jump in the first leaf pile
- your eyes lighting up at the first snowstorm of the year
- your hand reaching for mine first

you are my sweetest little shadow.
you go where I go,
even if you don't realize
it's the bathroom.
you want to taste what I eat
and help crack the eggs
when we make muffins.
if I brush my hair,
then you do, too.
you like to do all the chores with me,
and even though it takes twice as long,
I tell you that you are the best helper
I've ever had.

jessica jocelyn

you owe me nothing,
but I, on the other hand,
owe you the world.

I'm living with the sadness
of this stage ending
and the excitement of what's to come.
I want yesterday
and tomorrow so badly.

if I could keep you little forever,
I wouldn't.
as much as you are a part of me,
you don't belong to me.
you belong to the wind,
the moon, the stars.
your heart is going to change the world
and make it a better place.
and if I'm lucky,
I will be here to watch you do it.

the holidays this year
are so much sweeter.
you're finally old enough to understand
what's going on
and I welcome you into all
the new traditions.
I watch you hang ornaments
and I hold my breath
as you put them all in one spot
on the tree.
you turn back and smile at me,
so proud of what you've done.
it's beautiful, my love.
you make all the moments I'd enjoyed before
so much more special
and I get lost in the way
you help me believe in magic again.

mama, please be patient,
it's my first time here.

everything is new to me.
every sight, every sound.
please forgive the feelings
that can be too big for my tiny body.

I want to laugh and play
and do what you do,
and if I make a mess,
please forgive my tiny fingers
because it's their first time, too.

mama, please be patient,
I'm taking it all in
and learning how to be a person.
but I am so sure,
with all of my tiny heart,
that you will show me the way.

ever more

I held her hand the night
before she died
and whispered in her ear to not worry,
that we'd be okay.
she was my best friend,
but I didn't realize she was someone else's too.
my son just turned 3
and never had sleep issues before,
but he soon started coming into my room
at about midnight every night.
I'd hold him until he fell asleep
and then my husband would carry him
back to his room.
those were the moments I let myself grieve,
and not just for me, but for him.
he was so young,
I knew he wouldn't remember her soon.
I knew his little heart missed her
when the night terrors came;
they sounded just like my husband's.
my village- my sweet, loving village.
the woman who held my leg during birth,
the woman who taught me
how to change a diaper.
she was my homeland.
to do motherhood without her
was something I never expected.

each morning,
for 2 seconds, I forget that you are gone.
the realization sinks in
and the weight is so heavy.
I want to stay in bed;
I want the world to stop
just like your heart did.
but each morning, a tiny boy
comes into my room
and peeks up at me.
his eyes watch me fall,
but he also needs to watch me get back up.
so for now, I'll cry in the shower
and play games
while I am dying inside.
grieving while being a mother
is a luxury I can't afford.

each month I take a test,
and each month I shed tears.
there's a deep longing in my soul
as I feel ready for another baby.
my heart makes me give up
on taking those monthly tests
and then randomly I try again.
I am sure it will say negative,
as it has for years.
but there the lines are.
there is no maybe about it
the lines are bright and strong.
I put my hand to my belly
and know somewhere deep inside
someone very important is forming.

jessica jocelyn

the room is dark
and this time I'm hoping for a girl.
the wand glides over my belly
and we see the sweetest little profile.

*"are you ready?
it's another boy."*

my son yells out
"yes!! a boy!"
and high fives his daddy.

I feel a twinge of disappointment
but then I realize
I will be giving my son a friend for life,
a partner-in-crime.
even after I'm gone,
it will be him and his brother
against the world.

I have the best little hype man.
each week we sit
and look at the baby app together
and we try to find in the house
the object that the baby is now as big as.
sometimes we can't find it,
so we go to the store
and compare the object to my belly.
a fun scavenger hunt
that I hope he always remembers.

the small hands that rest on my growing belly
belong to a little boy
who's eager to meet the baby
growing inside.
for so long, it's been just us.
walking to the park,
watching movies,
reading books before bed.
all we know is this dynamic.
soon, there will be one more.
how incredibly amazing
that just as my body stretches
to make room for the new baby,
so my heart grows
to make room for him as well.

they say April showers
bring May flowers.
the storms can wear you down,
but what's on the other side
will always be worth it.
I may have trouble tying my shoes,
and sleep is hard to come by.
I have leg cramps when I wake up
and my joints feel so stiff.
I have trouble remembering things
and everything hurts.
but one day this will all be over,
and you'll be here, sweet baby.
my beautiful May flower
after all those April showers.

jessica jocelyn

they took you away
and I watched you from
the other side of the room.
you weren't crying.
I stopped breathing
and didn't start until you did, too.
they brought you back to me
and all I could focus on was your warmth.
I kissed your blue hands
and rubbed color back into them.
I never knew true fear until that moment,
and realized how scary it was
to love someone so much
that a part of me would die without them.

my son walked into the hospital room
wearing a shirt that said,
"keep the Earth clean, it's not Uranus"
with the solar system on it.
(planets were his special interest at the time)

I looked over at my husband and asked where
the cute outfit was that I picked out for him
because I knew I was going to take pictures
of him holding his brother
for the first time.

no one knew, of course.

my husband sat down with my oldest son on his
lap and my new son on his brother's lap.

"oh, mama, he's so bald! but that's okay, it will grow."

I went and sat back on the bed and stared
at all 3 of my boys.
it was one of the most precious moments
of my life.

(the shirt is now a favorite story for them to tell.)

I wasn't sure you were getting enough milk.
I'd never done this before
and you seemed to eat so often.
was it too often?
did that mean nothing was coming out?
my nipples were cracked
I didn't know I was supposed to
put that cream on them.
you were so patient with me,
the calm to the storm of worries inside me.
months later,
nice plump baby rolls told me
I was giving you enough.

my days are now filled
with nursing and pumping
and saying *"please use gentle hands"*
again and again,
with two separate bedtime routines
and a kindergartner bringing home viruses.
I binge watch SVU
in between pumping sessions
and adjusting to life
with a nursing newborn.
my hair all chopped off
because a pixie seems to make life easier.
some days it feels like I've added
5 children instead of 1
as I transition from 1 to 2.

there is peace in having
my second child.
I know how to change diapers
and have a system
to get my basic needs met.
I know how to set routines
and how to communicate better
with my husband
and make sure I am taking care of myself
so that I can better take care of the baby.
I know what to do when fevers spike
and not to rush milestones-
to let them come on their own time.
I know not everything needs to be perfect,
that I can allow myself to slow down
and soak in every baby moment I can
without rushing to mop the floors.

the baby can now sit by himself
and is starting to scoot around.
I catch glimpses
of the bond my sons share.
when my oldest son does silly things
just to hear his brother laugh
and how he pulls out his favorite books
and reads them to him.
he helps me throw away diapers
and helps cook baby food.
he wears his new big brother role
so proudly.

it was a normal, sunny summer morning
and I got up like normal before the boys.
I felt strange
so I grabbed a pregnancy test
from under the sink.
I didn't put too much thought
into the moment until there it was-

that second line.

immediately, thoughts from all directions
came flying at me.

I'm too old.
I just got rid of all my baby stuff.
I was ready to say goodbye to the baby phase.
I thought I was ready for the next phase
in our lives.

I walked in shock to the kitchen.
a notification buzzed on my phone-
a text from my husband that said
"*I thought about what you said;*
I think I'm ready to get snipped."

my oldest came into the kitchen holding my test.
I had been so shocked that I accidentally left the
test in the bathroom.

"*mama! I'm so excited. how many weeks?!*"
we got out a calculator and figured the due date
to be April 7, 2020.

April 7, 2020.
I'd have baby #3.
we'd be a family of 5.
ready or not,
a new baby was coming to join us.

jessica jocelyn

Part 2

jessica jocelyn

together
my husband and I cut into the cake.
when the knife comes out,
I see the pink frosting.
pink.
it's a girl.
deep down, I knew this time was different.
I haven't been as sick
and I still have my energy.
but now it's real.
a girl.
the responsibilities are now different.
I get to be for her
what I needed as a woman.
I get to be there in all those moments
to guide
and teach.

her first wound will not be her mother.

my boys are 4 and 9 and I'm 32 weeks pregnant.
my husband and I want to take them somewhere
fun to escape the bitter winter for a bit, so we
go to an indoor water park. our younger one is
still too small for the bigger waterslides so my
husband takes my older one and we stay behind
in the kiddie pool area.

I explain to him that I can't go down the slide
with him, that he has to do it himself and I will
be just feet away to catch him. he smiles and
screams as he scoots his little bottom and comes
down the slide. he goes faster than anticipated
and slips past me, but not before grabbing a
string from my bikini top. he ends up taking the
whole piece with him.

I am nearing the end of my pregnancy, so
hormones have taken control of my body and
my body has drastically changed in some areas.
and now all the middle-aged dads in the kiddie
pool area have seen my gigantic pregnancy
boobs. I cover them immediately with my hands
but it's too late and I have to grab the top from
my son. he gives it to me and tries to help me,
but all I can think is *I'm glad everyone is
pretending none of that just happened.*

tiny fingers glide over my big belly.
"when will the baby come, mama?"

I smile at him.
"soon, very soon."

his little face becomes worried.
"will you still love me?"

"of course. I am always going to love you.
I might be busy a lot
but you can always help me.
and just think.
when the baby is old enough to play,
you'll always have a friend."

his little fingers give my belly a pat.
"hurry up, baby.
we're gonna be best friends."

I feel the contractions start and I pull you close to me on the couch. we are watching a movie and I hum the songs in your ear. my arms are around you as the contractions start to burn more fiercely. I'm running out of time, but I want to take this moment in. I breathe you in and whisper *"I love you."*

my body is telling me your sister will be here very soon. and everything will be different. you won't be the youngest anymore. you won't be the baby anymore.

you will now be the middle child.
but you are so much more than that.
you are the bridge,
the one who connects the oldest and the youngest.
you are the baby I slowed down with,
the one who helped me learn
to just let the milestones
come on their own time.
the one to teach me patience
and bring me humility.

it's the first week of April, 2020. I am 3 days from my due date and we are driving to the hospital. my contractions are less than 2 minutes apart and I know that even though I am not in too much pain yet, she will definitely be here in the next hour. I know I'm running out of time.

before I get out of the car, I grab a mask and my husband grabs my bag and his. we have no idea if he's going to be able to come back inside if he leaves and we are terrified that he won't get to stay with me while the baby is being born. we walk quickly to the ER entrance and I tell them I'm in labor. everyone is wearing masks and they give my husband one. they ask how far along I am and take my temperature. I have a low-grade fever of 99° but by now I have my hands on my knees and I'm also wearing sweats. they take a step back and are very scared when they tell me about my fever. I tell them I'm just in labor and to please help me. they print me out a bracelet and get a wheelchair. I'm pushed to the maternity ward and they press a button to be buzzed in. nurses come to us and ask if we have an appointment. I'm now very annoyed and feel the contractions getting stronger. they tell me I need to stay in triage and I feel tears form in my eyes. I know my baby is coming, but the nurses are telling me they aren't sure if they can admit me.

they give me a gown and tell me they need to

weigh me. I start crying and look to my husband; I'm in so much pain, all I can say is *"help."* he comes over and undresses me and puts the gown on me. he walks me over to the bed and the nurse checks me.

"you're only 4 cm; I don't know if you can stay. we aren't keeping people in hospitals right now." and with that, she leaves me.

I start to panic. I rip off my mask. I have no room. I wanted to play Pink Floyd's "The Division Bell" on my little speaker. I wanted to give birth during the song "High Hopes." All I can do is breathe. I tell my husband I don't think I can do it without the epidural.

"Jess, there's no doctor. there's no one to get it for you. you wanted no drugs, remember? here, let's have you switch positions." he helps me stand and I feel my daughter lock into place in my hips. immediately my water rushes on to his shoes. the water is brown. the nurse comes in and her eyes bug out.

by now, I am yelling at the top of my lungs. a deep, low-toned yell. a noise I have never heard before. my body has taken over, I am no longer communicating or controlling my yelling. this is my third baby, but this is the first time without drugs. the nurse says I sound a little uncomfortable and tells me she's going to check me again. she then becomes terrified and says she needs to put an IV in immediately. she brings a clipboard and paper for me to sign. I grab the pen and drag it across the paper and slap it away. I stay as still as I can and take a deep breath so she can put the needle in my hand, but blood ends up everywhere.

they wheel me down the hall into another room and tell me to get on the bed. I'm concentrating on my baby moving through me and breathing but can't communicate other than shaking my head. my husband wraps his arms around me and lifts me. and there it is.

the ring of fire.
that's why they call it the ring of fire.

I lie on the bed on my side and I know her head is already out. the nurses gasp and tell me to stop pushing and that it's happening too fast. this angers me and in those 3 seconds, my baby and body became a team. I push and there she is, bloody, screaming, and as angry as I am.

immediately the pain is over.
my baby is here.
everyone is hesitant to touch us.
everyone is scared we could have covid.
my boys can't come meet their sister.
no visitors.
no flowers.

I ask them why my baby doesn't ever stay still and seems uncomfortable.
they tell me it's my fault because I had her too fast.
(turns out she has severe silent reflux)
we are out in under 24 hours.

ever more

one day,
there you were.
dropped from the sky
and placed on my chest.
we've known each other
for only a few minutes,
but the way you look at me
tells me we've known
and loved each other
in every single one of our lives.

2:00 a.m.
the baby cries in her bassinet.
she slept a little longer this stretch,
so my breasts are full, hard, painful.
it's much harder this time around,
being older than I was with my first.
I reach over, grab her,
and lift my shirt so she can smell me.
her mouth opens and hungrily she sucks,
drinking deep, gulping loud,
almost as if to say thank you.
I feel a hand on my shoulder.
"thank you for being her mother,"
my husband whispers as he looks at me.
I see his face in the moonlight,
his eyes full of helplessness.
it's not like it was the first time around.
our daughter refuses bottles
and all he can do is offer emotional support,
hand me water,
and wait to change her diaper.

here,
in this moment with you.
feeling your body soften
and rest all your weight onto mine.
the swooshing from your sound machine,
the gentle creak in the rocking chair.
knowing all is right in your world
makes everything right in mine.

jessica jocelyn

I'm running on 3 hours
of broken sleep.
I'm in an endless cycle of nursing
and diapers
and cleaning, cleaning, cleaning.
I grab pieces of food
when I can-
it might be the crusts from my toddler's toast
or maybe the pizza from last night.
we seem to be surviving
on a lot of that lately.
if my baby's eyes are open,
she is screaming at me.
I can't put her down,
so I wear her on my chest.
her reflux makes her angry all the time,
and sometimes I wonder
if it was anything I did during pregnancy
that gave it to her.
the doctors tell me the only thing
that will fix her is time,
but it's still so hard to see the light
at the end of the tunnel.

ever more

multitasking these days
looks like sitting on the couch
nursing the new baby
and eating a chicken sandwich
while reading a book
out loud to the boys.

my body is telling me it's done
the milk comes less and less.
soon there will be no more,
but I've decided that it's time.
we work hard together,
you and I,
to understand this new point in our lives.
we both shed tears
and it almost seems like we're not ready.
but we both know
it's time to move forward.

he is the bar
that she will set all other men against.
I watched it happen before my very eyes
the day my husband realized this.
I see it in every Valentine's Day
that he brings her flowers
and in the way
she climbs up beside him
and wrenches along some new project
he has started.
I see it in the way his voice has gotten softer
and the way he has changed for her.
she is his better days
and there is no bitterness in my mouth.
one of the greatest things I've ever given her
is a man who will not be her first heartbreak.

I think I yelled too much today.
I started my day
already running on empty
and kept taking from
what reserves I thought I had left.
turns out I had none
with just about as much patience.
when the day was done
and all the children were in bed,
all I could think about was
how much I had yelled.
I went back to each child,
kissed them on the cheek
apologized for losing my temper so much,
and said I loved them,
and tomorrow is a new day.
we get to start over
and have new adventures together.

ever more

this isn't the world
I thought I'd raise you in
and it's not the same world
I grew up in.
but if
all the stars ever fall into the sea,
the rains turn into fire,
and all the mountains crumble into dust,
you've got me.
until my time is done,
you've got me.

no one prepared me
for how it would feel
the day we disassembled
the crib for the last time,
knowing we'd never put it
back together again.
putting together the "new big kid bed"
for the last time.
putting away the highchair
for the last time.
knowing in our hearts
that the baby phase was over
and now we'd have to prepare
to watch our children grow into adults.
the saddest but most beautiful part
of this whole journey
is saying goodbye to one phase
and welcoming the next.

we are driving home from the store, just my youngest and me. I looked in the rearview mirror and saw she had fallen asleep. she was holding on to a pack of her new big girl underwear. we were officially out of diapers and having no accidents. she had been so excited to pick them out. she kept telling me she wasn't a baby anymore.

no you're not.
I don't have any babies anymore.
you were the last one.
I won't be changing any more diapers.

I think I'm okay until I feel the tears fall from my chin.

you are my last baby.

I'm sitting in my car.
I just ran some errands and now I'm back in my driveway. a playlist is still going strong, songs from the early 2000's because let's face it, they still hit me just as hard as the first time I heard them.

I look up at my house, feeling exhausted.
one more song, listen to one more song.
these stolen moments have become self-care. when it's just my thoughts and me.
these moments all alone.

the song ends, and as promised, I walk inside the house. my children hear me and I can hear them telling each other that I'm home. I walk into the kitchen and they run to me excitedly and tell me they missed me.

I feel guilty for needing a break from all this love, but sometimes, even love can get to be too much.

I walk into the living room and the kids are watching a cartoon from my childhood.

"hey, I remember when this episode first came out!" I told them.

my middle one looked at me and asked, *"was it in black and white?"*

"no! how old do you think I am?!" It felt like a moment to clutch my pearls.

my oldest started to laugh. *"calm down, Methuselah!"*

motherhood is being roasted by mini versions of you who happen to have the best burns.

one day I'm the Pinterest mom.
we sit down and all make crafts
that I thought of and we laugh
and hang them on the wall.

other days I'm the hot mess mom.
I'm hopping curbs at pick up,
Ozzy coming from my sound system
as the kids open the doors
while I yell *tuck and roll!*
and the only thing that rolls
are their eyes.

some days I'm the overstimulated mom.
I hide in the bathroom and eat alone
or take a shower and let out silent screams.
I snap at the kids and immediately
feel remorse that eats my soul.

but each day I am the present mom.
the one who always shows up,
the one who advocates
and protects at any cost.
the cornerstone,
the constant.

ever more

there are days (many days)
where I feel like I'm failing.

and then there are moments like these:

my daughter sat down to eat the last cookie. her brother came into the kitchen and with a tearful voice said *"oh there's no more cookies, I wanted one."* she looked at her cookie and with her small fingers, broke it in half and offered a half to her brother.

motherhood means long nights.
the nights when I slept
with my baby on my chest
to listen to him breathe when he had RSV.
the nights when I held them
until their fever broke,
because I was too scared to let go.
the nights when I stayed awake
and checked temps, and wiped noses
while they slept.
the nights when they couldn't sleep
because their coughing would keep them up.
and the many nights
with lots of cuddles
to chase away the terrors of bad dreams.

ever more

all 3 of my children
run through the pumpkin patch.
they each try to lift one
and outdo each other.
I remember when each of them
reached the "pumpkin" milestone
when they were growing inside me.
now here they are,
fighting over who can lift the biggest one.

every tear
that comes down your cheek,
I will wipe.
and every time
you look behind you,
I will be there
as long as you let me.

ever more

there are times
when I am so frustrated
that I have to take a step back
and remember that they are just children-
small humans with big feelings,
small humans that shouldn't be held
to adult standards.
they are allowed to be loud
and messy and make mistakes.
I need to be the adult
and help guide them
through regulating their emotions.
I was not given this grace as a child,
so I am learning to regulate
all these big feelings
right alongside them.

it's so healing to me
to watch my children
be loved in ways
that I wasn't.

ever more

my daughter watches me apply makeup
and says,
"mommy, I want to be pretty just like you."
I kneel to her and kiss her hands.
how can I explain to her that she
is a level of beauty I could never achieve?
she will be everything that I could not.
from the moment she was a seed,
I watered her even when
the only thing I had left to give was my tears.
I made sure the sun still shined
even when the storms surrounded me.
she is a fire that life can never stomp out
because she will be greater
than anything that tries.

my son,

I used to have to bend down
to pick you up.
your little arms reached up for me
your chubby fingers stretched wide.
now, I have to tilt my head upwards
and I'm not sure when that happened.
we used to sit and play with tiny cars
and now you help me carry in groceries
and make me laugh until I cry.
you have taught me so much
about life and myself.
we grew together,
you and I.
thank you
for the most beautiful journey
I have been on.

ever more

I'm cleaning up after dinner
while my husband chases our toddler
to get her to take a bath.
I finish and go wash her hair
and he starts cleaning the living room.
I get my toddler dried off and in pajamas
and prepare the bath for my middle one.
while he bathes, I make lunches
and my husband
keeps my daughter calm on the couch.
the nighttime energy kicks in however,
as all 3 children run around
laughing and screaming and then fighting.
through it all, we tag team
to make sure homework is done
and the teenager
doesn't sneak his phone to bed.
I take my daughter upstairs
while my husband gets the boys to bed.
there are endless requests for water,
the bathroom, and many books to be read.
we decide on 3 and I rock her while I read.
she tells me she doesn't want to sleep
but I softly stroke her nose
until she finally does.
I go downstairs and collapse
next to my husband on the couch.
we watch tv as we lie together,
knowing we're too exhausted to finish the show.
he kisses my head and it lets me know
that even after all this time,
we are still tag team partners for life.

jessica jocelyn

I used to wish
I could stay asleep
and be with my dreams.
now
being awake is better
and I couldn't
be prouder to say that.

I don't get to keep you forever
and my time with you is borrowed.
it goes so fast
but drags on all at the same time.
my heart exploded
the first time you wrapped your hand
around my finger,
and all through childhood,
we'd hold hands crossing the street
or even while watching a movie.
the hardest thing I will ever do
is learn to let you go,
but in my heart it will feel right
as I watch you use the very wings
I have given you.

I can't promise
that your life
will be without storms,
but I can promise
that I'll be there
holding an umbrella
teaching you
how to dance in it.

ever more

I am asked if I miss life
before my children,
or if I could do my life over,
would I have chosen differently?

instantly, my mind goes to moments
where I might say yes.
when it was just me to clean up after,
or when I need complete silence.
when there was no one else
for me to worry about
besides myself
or being able to just rest when I'm sick.

but what good is having all those things
if I were to still be who I was before?
lost in an implosive cycle of self-destruction.
what good is having all those things
if my heart never knew them?

so no, I wouldn't have chosen differently.
in the story of my life,
they are my favorite chapters,
my end-all be-all.
I owe every bit of who I have become
to the sacred souls
who call me mom.

jessica jocelyn

this is hard.
but I choose this hard.
I choose it as soon as I wake up
and even right before I go to sleep.
I chose it yesterday
and I will continue to choose it
until my body gives out.

I am a mother first.
my life has changed,
so I need to change along with it.

motherhood isn't a deep dark hole
although some moments
may try to convince me otherwise.
when I'm in the hole,
it's hard to humble myself
and ask for help.
I think I'm supposed to do it all,
but I have to remember
that it's never supposed to be that way.

maybe my body stays soft
so my children can
have a safe place to go.
they find respite in my curves
they find home
in my softness.

when I die,
I hope to turn into stars.
I hope to light up the night sky
so my children
can count all the twinkles I send them.

most of the time
I think I'm failing.
that maybe I'm not good at this
or it just wasn't something
I was meant to do.
that somehow everyone else
is doing much better.
sometimes all I want
is to know I'm not alone.
that other mothers struggle like I do.
that other mothers can't keep it
together all the time.

before I had children,
everything was a rush.
I couldn't wait to grow up.
I couldn't wait to finish college.
nothing ever seemed to go fast enough.
now, it's the opposite.
now, it seems I need life to slow down.
I need more hours in the day,
a moment to freeze,
to be fully submerged
in this new love I have.

before I had children,
I couldn't wait for time to pass.
now, I just wish it would slow down.

what did my parents teach me about love?
that it hurts.
it rips the skin completely off my bones.
that I give and I give and I give
until there's nothing left,
and still they'll ask for more.
that at the end of the day,
I am left completely empty
and I cry until I fall asleep.

what did my children teach me about love?
that it feels safe.
I can be myself and not be criticized.
that I can give and give and give
and there are tiny faces who look up at me
and say "mama, you're the best."
that at the end of the day,
I am so incredibly full
that if I cry, the tears don't drain me,
but rather they water my soul.

jessica jocelyn

I act like I am okay,
but deep down
I just want the village I was promised.
it hurts when
I watch all the grandparents
playing at the park
knowing my children
will never experience that.
my mother-in-law was gone too soon
and my own parents
couldn't be bothered.
anger burns from behind my eyelids,
forming hot tears
that I refuse to let fall.
my children may never know the love
of a grandparent,
but my future grandchildren absolutely will.

my life peaks with motherhood.
there are women
who tear me down
when they hear that.

but right here, in this morning,
making you cupcakes
for your birthday party,

I hope in every lifetime
I get to experience this.

people ask me what I do for a living.
I want to tell them I am..

a teacher.
a nurse.
a secretary.
a project manager.
a chauffeur.
a chef.
a therapist.
a librarian.
a maid.
a seamstress.
a personal shopper.
a tutor.
an accountant.
an event planner.
a construction worker.
a boo-boo kisser.

but I smile and say I am just a mother.

one day,
you'll ask me about these days.
the days when we rested skin to skin
and how you cried at every red light.
when we made forts with blankets and pillows
and how I cried on the first day of school,
but you didn't.
we'll get out your baby book
and read about each one of your birthdays.
we'll watch the DVD I made
of your baby shower
and I'll talk about how excited
everyone was to meet you.
I'll laugh and cry
and you'll ask if I would want to relive them.
I'll pause
but my answer would have to be no.
I lived every one of your stages to the fullest
and I don't think my heart could survive
saying goodbye to them a second time.

she sees the paint on the kitchen table,
but hours earlier everyone
made butterflies out of their hands
and hung the art on the fridge.

she sees the toys all over the floor,
but those blocks made castles
and a dragon came to blow them over-
imagination at its finest.

she sees the bathtub needs
to be cleaned,
but it only means
many deep-sea underwater adventures
took place there.

she sees a sink full of dishes
but meals were prepared
and bellies were filled.

she may see messes everywhere,
but she smiles
because childhoods are being lived.

ever more

it hit me,
on a random Sunday afternoon,
that I almost missed
these moments
and I am so thankful
the darkness of PPD
didn't win.

one day...
I will tell you how I was just like you.
how I couldn't wait to grow up
and would dream about
my future.
I'll tell you about how nervous I was
for the first day of high school
and how even more terrified I was
for my first day of college.
how the fears you have in your head,
feel the same in mine
and I understand you more than you think.
one day...
I hope to witness the magic
of the moment
you look into your child's eyes
and realize just how much I love you.

in this house,
we take mental health days from school.
we cry and we put on clothes that comfort us.
we apologize to each other
and discuss nightmares
till we remember they aren't real.
we dig for worms
and let snowflakes fall on our tongue.
in this house, we romanticize everything
and any achievement
is an amazing excuse for cake.
in this house,
my children know
they will always have a place
because this is their home, too-
they are not guests.
we hold one another close
and always remember
we end and begin with each other.

jessica jocelyn

I wish you could remember it, too.
the nights when it was just you and I,
hushed whispers and stolen lullabies.
you would fall and scrape your knee
and when you saw my face,
you felt safe enough to cry.
I wish you could remember it, too.
when my hugs and kisses
could solve any problem in your world
and calm your fears
of monsters in the closet.
I wish you could remember it, too,
those very early days.

just before
I close my eyes in death,
after a life well lived,
I'll have forgotten the way
I take my coffee
and I might have already
forgotten my name.
but just as my eyes are closing,
they will still search for a shadow
in the shape of your frame.
whatever journey my soul
goes to next,
I hope you'll be there.

she is not the same
and she never will be.
she is an indescribable masterpiece
woven from great pain
and unconditional love.
she is strength intertwined with softness.
she is louder,
        stronger,
                bolder.
all that she was before
is just a distant memory,
but she didn't mind leaving it behind
though she may look back fondly
from time to time.

mama,
I know you might feel
like you aren't good enough
or maybe your baby
is better off without you.
but that's not true.
it's not true today,
it won't be true tomorrow,
and it won't be true in 10 years.
you are the only one
who can love them the way you do.
you are the foundation, the glue,
and the most important person
in their world.
don't ever let your mind
try to convince you
that you don't belong
in the life that you created.
it isn't complete without you.

the hardships in
motherhood can come in waves.
one day you will be killing it,
absolutely killing it.
the next, you forget your child
had a half day at school
or had a dentist appointment that morning.
the waves will come.
the feelings of mom guilt.
inadequacy.
sensory overload.
lack of sleep.
when the big waves come,
give yourself permission to slow down.
remind yourself that you are amazing,
and the most important person
in the world to your children.
you practice so much patience with them,
it's time you gave yourself some, too.

children help you
still see the magic.
when their laughter fuels
your tired bones
as you see the same lava they do
and hurry to climb on the couch.
when you accidentally let go
of a balloon
and imagine that it goes to outer space
and makes little alien children happy.
when you leave out cookies for Santa
and you get so lost in the magic
that you almost believe
he's really coming.
children help you
still see the magic-
the magic that keeps our hearts young.

it's okay to say no.
no, you can't kiss my baby.
no, you can't hold my baby
without washing your hands.
no, you can't come over right now.
no, now is not a good time.

to all the mothers
whose oldest child
experienced the young, hurt,
unhealed version of themselves
that their youngest doesn't.
I see you.
I know how the guilt feels.
I know how hard you are trying
and see how far you've come.
I see the effort you put in
every day to not repeat mistakes.
and I'm proud of us.

jessica jocelyn

whenever you feel
that you are failing,
remember that to your child,
you are the moon,
the sun, and the stars.
the most important person
in the whole universe.

to the mothers who are breaking
all the cycles:

does cutting their sandwiches
into little shapes
heal you, too?

does it make your heart explode
to know you are the one they want
when they cry?

do you feel a sense of accomplishment
when they admit on their own
that they lied and they're sorry?

to all the mothers who are breaking
all the cycles:

you are amazing.

tell your children
who you were before them.
teach them your middle name
and how you spent summers
as a kid.
tell them what your biggest
and craziest dreams were,
what you liked to do
after school.
teach your children
all about you
and share all those moments
with them.

remember,
this is just a season,
and the season will pass.
sometimes it will roar through
like a cold bitter winter,
and sometimes it will slip by
like a February you won't recall.
but it will pass.
nothing lasts forever
and one day that screaming baby
will be a child who sleeps in
until you have to wake them up.
this is just a season,
and I promise one day you will sleep again.

"but you're the one who chose to have kids"

first of all,
how incredibly invalidating.
and secondly,
no one ever knows how incredibly hard it is
until you're in the thick of it.
expressing exhaustion
doesn't mean you don't love your children.
crying about the lack of sleep
doesn't mean you don't love your children.
feeling relief when you put them to bed
doesn't mean you don't love your children.
talking about the things your children do
that makes you upset
doesn't mean you don't love your children.

it is okay to express this.
you need to express it.
not expressing it manifests in your body
and can poison your heart and soul.

ever more

you are exhausted because
this is the hardest job in the world
and sometimes children can take
more love than they give.
you are exhausted because it's
a lot of work to love someone,
even more than you love yourself.
you are exhausted because
you are doing such an amazing job
even on days when you think you are not.

there is no manual
to parenting
and you are going
to constantly question yourself.
am I doing this right?
am I enough?
am I a good mother?
but I'm here to tell you
that 9 times out of 10,
if you are asking yourself these questions,
it means you are a good mother.
and 10 times out of 10,
you are enough.

you are a good mother.

ever more

may I live up
to everything
my children think I am.
may I always be worthy
of the love
that I see in their eyes.

jessica jocelyn

ABOUT THE AUTHOR

Jessica Jocelyn is the author of four poetry books (Chasing Wildfires, Finding Daisies, Girl (Remastered) and Ever More), a proud mother, and a nemophilist. By sharing her lived experiences, she strives to deeply connect with her readers and remind them that they are not in this alone. Jessica's poetry may be hard to hear at times, but it's always healing to read. In the same vein, her past may be dark, but writing serves as her spark of sunlight. When she isn't storytelling, you can find this free-spirited goth spending quality time with her family that inspire her every day.

instagram: @letters.to.anna
tiktok: @jessica.jocelyn

other titles by the author:

the journey of loving an addict

chasing wildfires

jessica jocelyn

the author's personal journey of the building, destruction, and reconstruction of a family effected by addiction told through poetry.

ever more

jessica jocelyn

finding daisies

decorations by
janelle parraz

poetry on healing the inner child and
breaking the cycle

jessica jocelyn

> jessica jocelyn
>
> encontrando
> margaritas
>
> decoraciones de janelle parraz

the Spanish version of Finding Daisies

girl (remastered)

jessica jocelyn

poetry on childhood trauma, toxic relationships, motherhood, religious trauma, and late autism diagnosis

jessica jocelyn

Made in the USA
Columbia, SC
08 March 2024